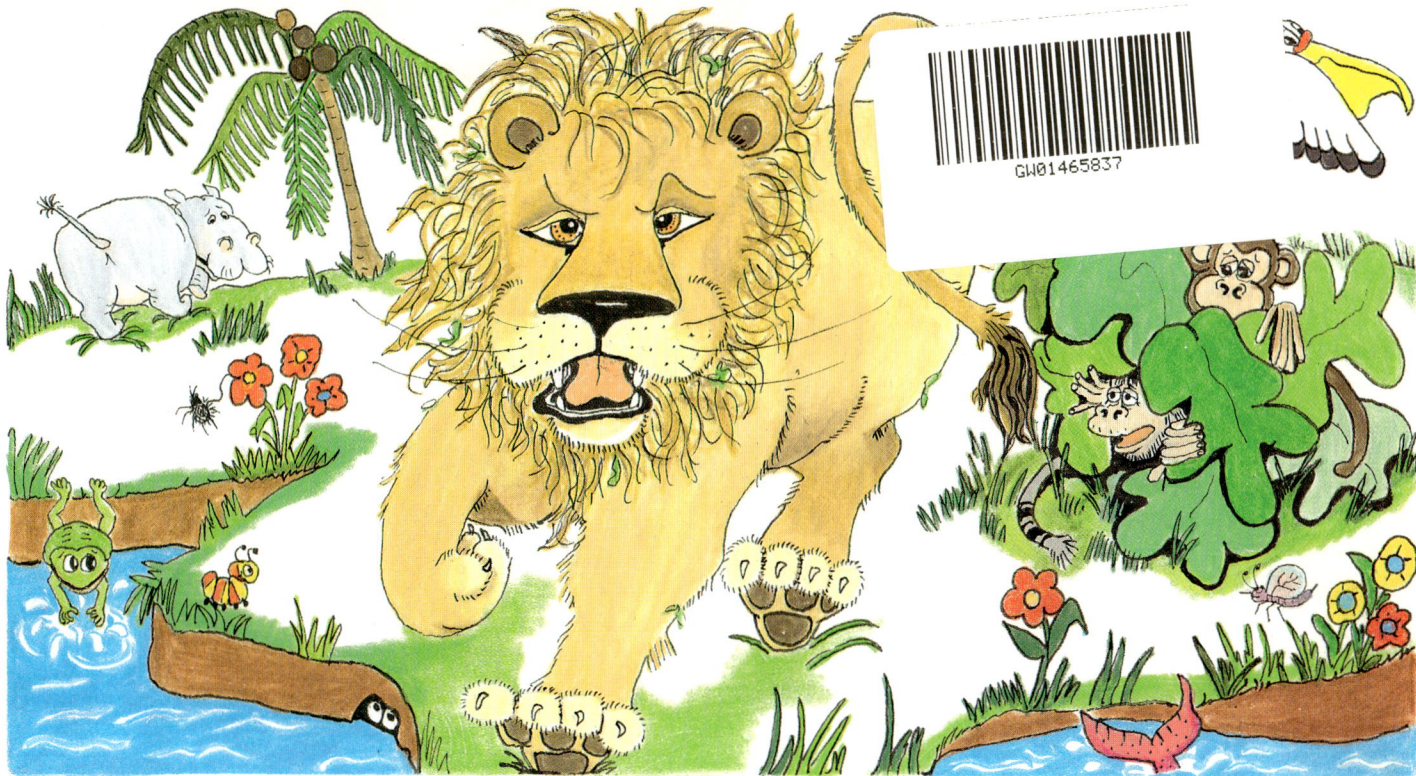

"Out of my way everyone," roared the Lion as he wandered down to the lake. The other animals soon scampered off when they heard him coming.

1

When Lion had finished drinking he looked at his reflection in the water. "Why am I so ugly?" he thought.

He moved his head from side to side. Then he climbed on to a
rock to get a better view of himself.

The sky became dark. Spots of rain splashed on the water and
soon Lion could not see his reflection.

This was too much for him and he roared as loud as he could. Then he sat down in a puddle.

5

All the other animals gathered round. They asked if there was anything they could do to help for Lion was, after all, the King of the jungle.

"I'm so ugly," cried Lion, as he buried his head in the bushes.

"Why don't we give him a bath?" said Pelican, "and make his mane curly."
"All right," said Lion, "but please don't hurt me."

Lion sat very still. Hippo washed him and the monkeys tied up his mane with reeds and grass.
When it was dry they put a crown on his head.

Lion ran to the water. "Just look at me, I'm much better looking than I thought," he said. Of course all the other animals agreed.

For several days Lion was kind to everyone but then it started to rain. It rained so hard that everyone got very wet.

"Look at me, I'm ugly again," roared Lion and his crown fell off into a puddle. The other animals were frightened and hid in the trees.

"Come back, come back," cried Lion, "I won't hurt you." Gradually they returned.

"This won't do, said Monkey. "Every time it rains Lion gets angry. Every time we make him beautiful we risk being eaten."

"I know what we can do," said Pelican. "Lion is our King and he should live in a palace. We will build him one by the lake so that when it rains he can keep himself dry. When it's fine he can look at his reflection in the water."

So they built him a fine palace and made a roof with large green leaves. They put flowers in the window and dry leaves on the floor.

Lion became the happiest animal in the forest.